When I Am the Leader . . .

Fannie T. Brown

Order this book online at www.trafford.com
or email orders@trafford.com

Most Trafford titles are also available at major online book retailers.

Printed in the United States of America.

ISBN: 978-1-4669-0216-9 (sc)
ISBN: 978-1-4669-0212-1 (e)

Library of Congress Control Number: 2011919113

Trafford rev. 01/11/2012

 www.trafford.com

North America & international
toll-free: 1 888 232 4444 (USA & Canada)
phone: 250 383 6864 ♦ fax: 812 355 4082

Table of Contents

About the Author

Fannie T. Brown is a native of Bladenboro, N.C. She grew up in this small town, where she enjoyed farming and fishing. Most of all, she enjoyed reading to younger children and helping them with their home work. The children soon coined these tutorial sessions as "Play Teacher."

After completing high school, she attended Winston-Salem Teacher's College, now known as Winston-Salem State University, which is located in Winston-Salem, N.C. After graduating in 1965, she moved to Myrtle Beach, S.C., where she became a permanent resident. She began teaching in Horry County Schools, while undertaking graduate work at the University of South Carolina.

After retiring from Horry County Schools in 1996, she decided to "Play Teacher," once again, for younger children by writing children's books. Her books incorporate poetry, illustrations, fun-filled facts, and a teaching methodology that facilitates material comprehension and material retention, for young children. To date, she has produced the following titles:

Who is President?
Where Are the Children?
When I Am the Leader . . .
What About Your States?
Why This?

When I am a leader

When I am a leader . . .

I am a very young child,
but I know I am on my way,
to become a great leader some day.

As I travel through life,
there are many great leaders I will see.
But, no one can really say,
what leader is best for me.
Only I can determine,
the leader I will be.

Parent

Parent . . .

Parents are the first leaders,

we will probably see.

They always want us to be,

the best that we can be.

They love us, and they care for us.

They give us advice and show us the way.

Parents know that loving and caring,

will help us become a great leader someday.

Teacher

Teacher . . .

Are teachers good leaders?
"Yes," of course, "I think so!"
Teachers try to lead me,
in the ways that I should go.

Teachers gather information,
and put it at my fingertips.
As I search for the leader I will be,
teachers will prepare me for my trips.

Principal

Principal . . .

A principal is a leader.

A principal is the head of a school.

He is the chief executive officer.

He is the one who sets the rules.

The principal makes sure,

the information is there,

so that all students are able to,

learn, lead, and share.

Superintendent

Superintendent . . .

The superintendent of schools has executive oversight of
many schools.

The superintendent is in charge of setting the rules.

The superintendent makes sure the schools have the
resources they need,

to provide the skills and experiences children need to succeed.

The superintendent is the leader,

I know I will be.

"Please don't ask me when."

"You just wait and see!"

Mayor

Mayor . . .

The mayor is an elected leader,
of a town, a city, or borough.
He will study the laws, the policies,
and the budget, very thorough.

The mayor will study the city plans very carefully.
He will move the city in the direction,
of where it needs to be.
The mayor will try to make improvements,
for the city residents to see.

Councilman or Councilwoman

Councilman or Councilwoman . . .

A city councilman is an elected leader.
He is a leader that the city residents have sent,
to represent them,
in "city government."

If you leave a "city" and keep going,
you will enter into the "county,"
without knowing.
A county councilman is the elected leader,
the county residents have sent,
to represent their interest,
in "county government."

Governor

Governor . . .

The governor is an elected leader.

He controls, directs, and strongly influences,

the actions of the state.

I think this may be,

the kind of leader I will make.

If this is the leader,

I know I want to be.

I must begin, now,

setting goals, for me.

Lawyer

Lawyer . . .

Once, there was a great leader I saw,

whose profession was to practice the "law."

He was a lawyer and he gave "legal advice."

He represented his clients in court,

without even thinking twice.

To be like this lawyer,

would be so nice.

A lawyer is the leader I will be,

I know I am willing to "pay the price."

Judge

Judge . . .

A judge is a public official.
He is the leader in charge of the court.
When issues are brought before a court,
the "sitting judge" will decide.
The judge gives his opinion,
and everyone in court must abide.
Remember! When trials are over,
at the end of the day,
what matters most,
is what the judge will say.
The leader I will be,
is a judge, someday.

Secretary

Secretary . . .

When I am the leader,

I will be a secretary.

I will send a friendly note,

to give someone in desperate need, "hope."

I will record a special speech,

that an important person spoke.

I will send special greetings,

to inform people of meetings.

I will keep good records.

So, people will not have to worry,

when I am the secretary.

Attorney

Attorney . . .

An attorney is a leader,

who is legally appointed by "you,"

to transact your business,

that may be too difficult for you to do.

When I become an attorney,

as I go through life searching to find my way,

maybe someone will appoint me,

to handle their "legal business" some day.

Police

Police . . .

A police officer is a member of a police force,

whose duty is to keep everyone on "course."

A police officer enforces the laws,

detects, and prevents crimes.

Oh! I think I will be a police officer,

I have said so many times.

When I am a leader, such as a police officer,

I will protect everyone from crimes;

and, I will bring peace and comfort to their minds.

District Attorney

District Attorney . . .

The prosecuting officer for a judicial district is a district attorney.

When law officials are trying to make a "case,"

this can be a long fought journey.

Investigators must visit crime scenes to gather information,

for the district attorney to see.

The district attorney must decide,

what the "case" will be.

Will this information be enough,

to withstand objections and lots of "stuff?"

Now, I know a district attorney,

is the leader I will be.

Attorney General

Attorney General . . .

An attorney general is the chief law officer of a nation or a state.

The attorney general must "know what it takes,"

to represent the government in legal matters,

with very few errors and no mistakes.

When I am the attorney general,

I will be the government's principle legal advisor, you see!

So, an attorney general,

is the leader I must be.

Representative

Representative . . .

A representative is a typical example,
of a group of people that is ample.
Usually, chosen by an election,
he or she speaks on behalf of a group's sample,
from a particular section.
When I am a representative,
I will be a member of the "House of Representatives,"
within the United States Congress.
I will more or less fulfill
the people's interests and objectives.
I will represent my state,
and I will keep the state up-to-date,
on issues that are taking place,
and problems my state may face.

Congressman or Congresswoman

Congressman or Congresswoman . . .

A congressman or congresswoman,
is the leader I will be.
I will be as busy as the bees,
when they are making sweet honey.

I will help to make the laws,
that effect every citizen.
I will also decide how the government spends its money,
and how it provides benefits.

Senator

Senator . . .

A senator is the leader I will be!
So, while I am waiting to become thirty,
I must do good things for people to see.
I will make sure the people,
in my state really, really care,
about the things I have to say,
and what I have to share!

I will be a member of the senate,
that forms the government's ability to "check and balance,"
the powers of the elements, in the federal government.
But, I may advise and consent,
to the President's government appointments.

Supreme Court Justice

Supreme Court Justice . . .

Maybe the Supreme Court Justice,

is the leader I will become.

I will make sure that justice,

for the United States is done.

When I am a Supreme Court Justice,

I will have so many things to do.

I will make sure the Constitution,

is carried through for you.

Secretary of State

Secretary of State . . .

When I am the leader,
Secretary of State is the leader I will be.
I will thank the President of United States,
for appointing me,
as the smartest person,
in "foreign policy."

I will conduct negotiations,
relating to United States' "foreign affairs."
I will make sure my decisions are those,
the American people share.

Vice President of the United States

Vice President of the United States . . .

When I am the leader,

the Vice President of the United States,

is the leader I will be.

I will be the head of the "Senate,"

where we may set legislation limits,

I can only vote if there is a "tie."

That is part of my duty,

so, no one should question, "why?"

If the "President" can no longer serve as President,

I will become President,

although I am not the person,

the people originally sent.

President of the United States

President of the United States . . .

When I am the leader,
President of the United States,
is the leader I will be.
I will be the leader of the United States,
from "sea to shining sea."

I must always do my duty.
I must always do my best,
to make America a better place,
and I hope "Congress" will do the rest.

I will be Head of State,
and I will lead the Government.
But, I must always remember,
I am the leader the "people" have sent.

NOTES

NOTES

NOTES

NOTES

NOTES

NOTES

NOTES

NOTES

NOTES

NOTES

NOTES

NOTES

NOTES

NOTES

NOTES

NOTES

NOTES

NOTES

NOTES

NOTES

NOTES

NOTES

NOTES

NOTES

NOTES

NOTES

NOTES

NOTES